a to Z

Interior Decoration
a to Z

BETTY PEPIS

DOUBLEDAY & COMPANY, INC.
GARDEN CITY, NEW YORK

By the same author

BOOKS IN YOUR HOME
BETTY PEPIS' GUIDE TO INTERIOR DECORATION
HOUSE AND GARDEN GUIDE TO INTERIOR DECORATION
BE YOUR OWN DECORATOR
LE GUIDE PRATIQUE DE LA DECORATION
THE PERSONAL TOUCH IN INTERIOR DECORATING

Interior decoration is the mid-twentieth century's contribution to the arts of living. For only in our own time has the planning, placement, and selection of furnishings been dignified by being deemed a profession.

Indeed the oldest professional organization of decorators in the United States (who today prefer to be called designers in the belief that this latter word is more all-encompassing) dates back to 1931. And Elsie de Wolfe, later Lady Mendl, who, perhaps somewhat inaccurately, has been called the first interior decorator, turned to this vocation around the turn of the century and did her most important work in the years just preceding 1920.

Prior to this period and to a certain extent even up to the 1930s, decorating, per se, was for the rich who relied for help, guidance, and instruction upon architects or a superior breed of craftsmen: cabinet-makers of the caliber of Chippendale and Hepple-white in England and in our own country, Duncan Phyfe.

Men such as these set fashions, created a certain over-all look. But it was not one to which the average householder could aspire. The style-oriented furniture store and decorating sections of department stores, both catering to the many rather than the few, are of reasonably recent vintage and it is these along with the growing number of individual decorators who have evolved the pattern of making fashion important in the home.

In line with this development a whole new vocabulary has come into being. Because practitioners of this very contemporary profession compile as well as create, words have been borrowed from adjacent arts (painting and architecture, to name only two) and given new application and meanings. Other words and phrases have been manufactured to suit situations peculiar to modern residential design. Open floor plan is one example. Room divider and clerestory are others.

5

Modern technology and engineering have contributed too. Cantilevered chests and molded chairs are among contemporary additions to the elements of interior design—and not in name only but in concept as well.

Probing the past for inspiration has resulted in the excavation of terms that were for a time out of use, and had lost meaning for the average amateur, who, ten years ago, might not have known or cared what the difference was between an epergne and an *étagère*, or between a galloon and a gadroon. Today, all four might pertain to the furnishings of a simple living room.

Increased travel and more intensive international communication have lead to broader knowledge and acceptance of arts and crafts from various parts of the world. As a result, rya rugs share space with sliding shogi, and though neither word has been widely known, both are frequently applied to room designs today.

The well-dressed room has become a status symbol denoting knowledgeability and sophistication, outranking in importance, at the moment, even the compact foreign car. As such, it invites analysis in somewhat abstract terms, and each of the taste-making authors has come up with his or her own newly coined definition of, for example, elegance.

This book is designed as a visual guide through the maze of words from many sources that make up the vocabulary of modern interior design. A perusal of it will inevitably result in recognition of the trends of the times (a much more complex matter than at any period of the past), for the words simply define the increasingly varied elements that contribute to contemporary decoration.

ACCESSORIES. Little things that make a big difference in the total effect of interior decorating. Taking up where the larger elements of backgrounds and furnishings leave off, they offer the opportunity for uninhibited expression of personal taste. Included in this category are even flowers and plants.
With dramatic impact, a profuse flower arrangement as that below picks up the colors and enhances the importance of an old Moroccan rug, a contemporary ceramic plaque, two other important accents in the room. Collected at right are a number of modern hand-crafted contemporary items, any one of which could add character to a room. They show the range of materials explored by contemporary craftsmen: metal and ceramic, enamel, stained glass, colored plastic (in the woven hanging).

Accessories. Machine-made objects and many imports supplement hand-crafted accents in rooms of today. Among their more notable contributions is the vivid, smashing color they can add. Strikingly brilliant examples are the red lacquer table, orange glass bowl at left. Imports also add a special flavor; included here are a gilded bird from Burma, a delicate screen from Japan, and lacquer boxes from that country, a Danish red glass cylinder performing as a lamp base, an old Chinese lacquered leather box, Moroccan lantern wrought of brass and stained glass. Accessories, because they are small, can be blatant in color and quite exotic in flavor for greater impact.

11

Accessories. Large pieces of colored furniture are among the most popular of these in use today and may be found in all of the period styles as well as the contemporary versions like the vitrine, tall chest, and small three-legged table seen here. Colonial chairs with mustard or slate-blue frames, French *bergères,* pastel-tinted, and with upholstery to match the watery blues, pale greens and apricots, stark modern cube tables in primary tones of red, yellow, or blue are other devices that can add excitement to decorating a room.

Accessories. Accouterments for dining are included among these and serve a most important purpose in brightening the home. They are more colorful than ever before in history: printed cloths, harmonizing napkins, platters, and plates that pick up a room's scheme all add up to a dashing informality that is in line with today's casual living and is a far cry from the stiff damasks, tall stemware, and decorated plates once popular.

Accessories. Serving pieces should not be overlooked when assembling the essentials of decorating. Emphasis on home entertaining makes these an important part of decoration, and selection should conform with all the other elements of decoration. Outdoor events, as well as indoor ones, deserve consideration. Release from the onetime binding conventions has made it possible, in recent years, to exert as much play of imagination in choosing these as in picking out any other type of accessory for decorating.

ADAM STYLE. Style devised by two English architects (brothers) in the late eighteenth century. Furniture designed by them has a certain delicacy, is much infused with the classicism of Rome, is often painted or veneered in unusual woods (satinwood, for example). Table here is typical.

ADAPTATION. Furniture that captures the spirit of a period without exactly duplicating the precise measurements or motifs. The dining room table and chairs at right are based on originals found in Williamsburg, Virginia and dating from the eighteenth century. Dimensions are smaller.

ALCOVE. Small room off of a larger one. Most often put to use to contain a bed. Today, a much used device to conceal sleeping quarters during daytime hours, but can also be effectively adapted as a book-lined study area.

AMERICANA. The folk-art of our American forefathers is so called. Includes such whimsies as weathervanes and shop signs as well as paintings, prints, carved wood figures.

ANTIQUE. Anything old, old according to the United States Customs Office being an object made before 1830. Applies to made-in-America furnishings and art like that shown here or importations from abroad including accessories.

ANCIENT. Considerably older than antique, dating in actuality to antiquity like this Islamic jar, which was made in the seventh or eighth century. A Greek urn, an Egyptian figurine also fit in this category.

(COURTESY MUSEUM OF MODERN ART)

APPLIQUÉ. A decoration that is applied to another surface. It can be three-dimensional such as a sconce or wall clock or lacquer added to metal, or refer to cutouts of one fabric sewn on top of another.

APRON. One way to dress up a battered tabletop— preferably a round one such as that at left. Mostly made of stiff fabrics like taffeta or velvet and always with a floor-length hem. More technically, an apron is a piece of wood set at right angles to the underside of a table as illustrated below.

ARCHITECTURAL DETAIL. Those additions to box-like rooms which give some distinction to the pared-down simplicity of so many homes and apartments of today. Although they appear to be of structural significance, they are purely decorative, not functional. The moldings here are one example. Other types follow.

Architectural detail can be painted on, following earlier traditions of France and Italy. Even the ceiling has been so treated in the dining room at left which one approaches through doors painted to simulate marble. This treatment is more appropriate in a traditional than a modern room. Not-so-classical columns were architectural detail added to the room at right. They seem to support the arches above the windows, although they do no such thing. They do, however, serve to give importance to the window bay and create a frame for a spectacular view.

ARMOIRE. Tall cabinet with doors, meant for hanging clothes. Can supplement closets when there are too few. Modern interpretations are showing up.

ARTIFACT. Article of great age, made by man in an earlier civilization. Valued for its antiquity. These Peruvian pots supported on brackets are typical.

ART MODERNE. Style that flourished in France during the 1920s, then put in a brief appearance in the United States. Much under the influence of cubist painting as seen in the rug at left.

ART NOUVEAU. Protest movement that broke away from the precedents of past periods and reached out for new expressions in decoration. The florid floral above shows the preference for a swirling line also illustrated in the interior at right. Established around 1900 and popular again.

ART WALL. The current craze for collecting art, often much of it minor, has led to the development of this taste for massing many pictures in a single composition on a wall. The impact they can have when presented in such formation can be as dramatic as that of a single stunning masterpiece of a large size. The advantage of this approach: it permits the inclusion of artworks not strong enough to stand on their own, and a mixture of many types of media is possible. Four examples are shown here.

ARTS AND CRAFTS. Often used to soften the severe, strict lines of modern furniture, these hand-fabricated objects may be made of many materials: of pottery, of woven reeds, of twisted wire as seen above. On occasion, they are useful, as is the perforated ceramic lantern below; at other times—simply meant for decorative effect.

ASYMMETRIC. Kind of arrangement
that achieves a sense of balance
through the use of harmonizing sizes
and styles rather than matched pairs of
tables, chairs, or lamps. A good example is
the living room above in which the
principle is accentuated by the off-center
placement of the coffee table balanced
by a pile of pillows. Such a carefully
composed setting seems more pleasing in
modern rooms than stiff regimentation.

AVANT-GARDE. Style of decoration that disregards the precedents of the past; forecasts for the future. The startling setting, left, is a case in point. The living room of a well-known architect, it is an experimental study in the use of plastics. Sheets of white plastic sheath the walls, are used for tabletops supported by slabs of clear plastic. Eventually these far-out ideas can find acceptance. The concept of cushions on a platform for seating seemed daring in 1952 (top right). Today it has become a favored fashion. See the two rooms, right.

AUTHENTIC. Either the original antique or a precise copy of it. In the case of this chair, both exist. The prototype, now in a museum in Paris, celebrated the balloon ascension of the Montgolfiers.

BALUSTER. An upright member, often in an elongated urn shape as above, used to support a handrail. Commonly used as an accompaniment to stairs but equally effective as a device to define and mark off a section of a room.

BAMBOO. Not necessarily made from the actual branches of this tropical plant are the many handsome chairs one sees. Imitations in wood of these shapely stalks, popular ever since the eighteenth century, unlike the real thing won't warp or split in steam-heated rooms.

BAROQUE. Large scale, bold detail, and sweeping curvilinear lines are characteristic of this style, which originated in Italy in the sixteenth century. Despite its fascination, it has little application today because of these decidedly imperious qualities.

BANQUETTE. Seating setup built in along a wall and specifically planned for use while eating. A way to achieve an air of both opulence and intimacy in even the tiniest dining area. The mural, here, draped like a window, adds glamor.

BASKETS. Objects woven of reeds, handmade around the world, have acquired acceptance as proper appurtenances for the home. Sometimes they make surprising switches: a fish basket, for example, converts to a lamp and a storage trunk turns up as a coffee table.

BEADS. These many splendored bits of cork, wood, crystal, and now even plastic, add drama to doorways or windows, can be hung from the ceiling to serve as room dividers. Used in the Near and Far East for centuries, they add a subtly exotic touch to a modern room.

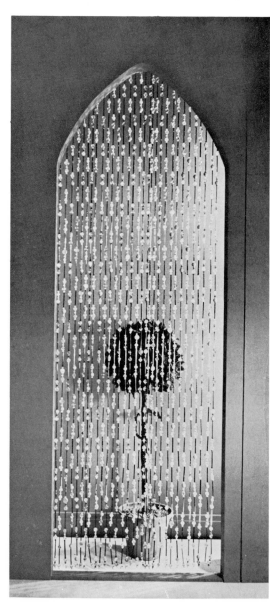

BELTER. Cabinetmaker by the name of John, whose carefully curved and carved rosewood pieces represent about the finest type of American Victoriana. Pierced frame, high relief trim of this 1850 chair are typical.

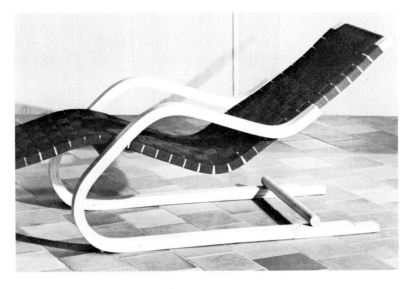

BENTWOOD. Bending wood was a technique developed in late nineteenth-century Europe. It streamlined both the manufacture of chair design (as in the frame, here, made of only two pieces of wood), and the basic design.

BERGÈRE. Actually the French word for a shepherdess, but applied to armchairs in various French styles designed to accommodate the exaggerated side-paneled skirts of these rural ladies. Inside of arm is upholstered.

BIBELOT. More than a trinket, more than a toy (the two conventional definitions). Proof of the statement that good things come in small packages, perfume bottles and miniature boxes are among these collector's items.

BIEDERMEIER. Furniture style named after a cartoon figure in mid-eighteenth-century Vienna. A little plump, a little pompous, but amply endowed with the famed Viennese charm, it can be updated as seen below.

BOMBÉ. Shape of a chest which bulges out lusciously in the center front and makes secondary small dips at the sides. Characteristic of sophisticated Parisian chests of the time of Louis XV— and also Provincial.

BRUTAL. Not derogatory as one might expect but simply descriptive of a kind of architectural (and interior) design that esteems the use of natural unpolished materials such as in this stony, cave-like room.

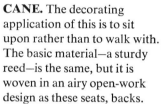

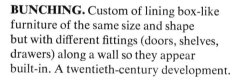

BUNCHING. Custom of lining box-like furniture of the same size and shape but with different fittings (doors, shelves, drawers) along a wall so they appear built-in. A twentieth-century development.

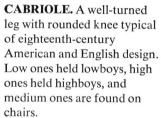

CABRIOLE. A well-turned leg with rounded knee typical of eighteenth-century American and English design. Low ones held lowboys, high ones held highboys, and medium ones are found on chairs.

CANE. The decorating application of this is to sit upon rather than to walk with. The basic material—a sturdy reed—is the same, but it is woven in an airy open-work design as these seats, backs.

CAMPAIGN FURNITURE. Portable, collapsible furniture of a type contrived for Napoleon's officers on their marches. Chests come apart, chairs fold up as do bedsteads. Translated into modern forms like those illustrated here: good for families on the move.

CANOPY. Drapery suspended over any piece of furniture. Could be a sofa, but more often is a bed, where its original purpose was to provide protection against both enemies and drafts. Although both objectives appear to be obsolete, decorative values remain.

CANTILEVER. Structure sticking out from a wall with no apparent means of support. A twentieth-century architect's device to hang balconies on a building, that has been adopted for hanging shelves, chests, and other storage units by interior designers.

CARYATID. Column with a recognizable female conformation used to hold up a top of sorts. The Greeks, who had this word for it, used these intriguing supports for temple roofs. In the early nineteenth century, when interest in the Golden Age ran high, the ladies reappeared under tables.

CASEMENT CLOTH. Derives its name from the type of window that opens in or out on hinges rather than pushing up and down. Specifically refers to open, airy weaves well suited to walls that are all window, for they filter light without looking especially heavy.

CASTER. Those small wheels that make it possible to push around heavy pieces of furniture like tea carts or even sofas. First used in the early nineteenth century but even more popular today. The same term describes a glass container for condiments.

CASUAL. Much-used, much-abused term designating a room geared to informal living, relying on sturdy, easy-to-maintain materials, such as bare, painted, planked floors, metal frames, washable or washoffable fabrics. Misinterpreted to mean just careless.

CERAMIC. Clay contributes many varied ingredients to the arts of decoration. Combine earth with fire and you can come up with ordinary brick, old or new, or a handsomely textured wall (left). The same ingredients handled differently will produce delicate hand-crafted bowls. Three more applications are included in the room at right: a shiny white tiled floor, a tabletop of multicolored squares and hanging lanterns pierced and finished with flower-like designs. Because of their alliance with the earth, all work very well out-of-doors.

CHAISE LONGUE.
Elongated chair with a firm support for the back. Once it was confined to bedroom usage; now, however, such a substitute for a chair plus ottoman respectfully can put in an appearance in the living room. A pair can look particularly handsome jutting out on two sides of a hearth.

CHANDELIER. Evolved from the French word for candle, this word has come to mean any lighting device that dangles from the ceiling. Variations devoid of the conventional prisms are shown here in Spanish-styled black iron, antique French crystal, modern American plastic.

CHIC. Understated, up-to-date approach to interior decorating, as in this all-white bedroom with its few carefully selected pieces. Opposed to chi-chi, which is effete, affected.

CHINOISERIE. Decoration done not by the Chinese but in imitation of them. Can be paint or lacquer. Much appreciated in eighteenth-century Italy and also in England.

CHINTZ. Fabric with a floral design and shiny surface. Now much in favor for use with traditional English designs of the eighteenth century, although back in that time the shine may not have been present. Not to be confused with "chintzy," a slang word for "corny."

CHIPPENDALE. Most famous of all the eighteenth-century English cabinet makers. Studied and adapted many cultures, including both Gothic and Chinese.

CLERESTORY. Term borrowed from church architecture to describe windows placed high on the wall of a building, permitting both light and ventilation to enter without breaking into the lower portion of the wall. A frequently seen design technique in contemporary homes where these under-ceiling strips of window often face whole walls of glass.

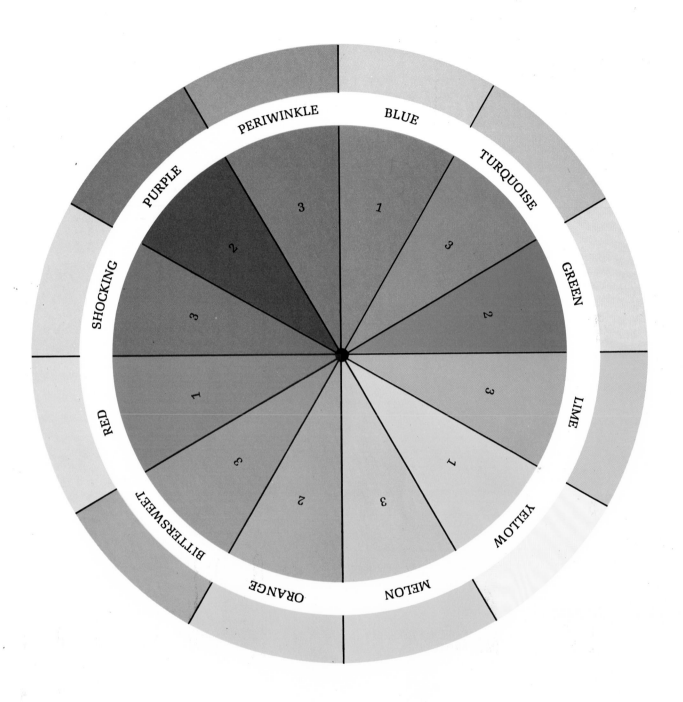

COLOR. The most inexpensive asset
in all of decorating. The color wheel,
above, a rainbow in circular form, is the
basis of good color planning, shows
the relationship of one color to another.
It provides the clue to four basic schemes
described in the following pages.
They are called by name: monochromatic,
analagous, complementary, and triadic.

49

Color. Clues for color schemes derive from a great range of inspirations, can come from a painting, a printed fabric, or more unexpectedly, from a piece of furniture such as the small round Venetian chest below which suggested the pastel scheme ranging from pale to vivid. From the floral painting on its façade were chosen the greens, golds, and intense corals of the fabrics and accessories, all underlined by earth tones of the rya rug.

Fan-shaped vase of Tiffany glassware, below, has the
brilliant peacock-feather hues, encouraged the creation of
a daring and off-beat scheme, its richness emphasized
by the inclusion of golden brass accents. The stained glass
tones are given further definition by the addition of
touches of fuchsia and the jolting surprise note of the
turquoise blue hexagonal floor tiles. A lacquered screen or
box could start another scheme.

Color. Monochromatic schemes, based on the color wheel, are composed of tints and shades of a single color. Because of their simplicity, they are highly sophisticated. And because there is little color variation (black and white and neutrals do not count), variation of texture becomes all important to avoid monotony. Using them takes semi-professional skill. Any of the twelve colors shown on the wheel may be handled in such fashion. Dull tones such as the deepened golds, left, or bright ones such as the corals below lend themselves equally well to this kind of treatment. Touches of white in both cases leaven the effect of undiminished, undiluted color.

Color. Analagous schemes make use of
colors that are side by side on the
color wheel on page 49. They have become
the rage in recent years, making use as
they do of modern-looking, color-clashing
tones. They can give a contemporary lift
to traditional rooms, and because the
guide lines are so positive, are easy to work
out. Orange walls keynote the brilliant
color planning conceived here. Surrounding
it on the color wheel are the sharp hues
of the orange-red covering on some of the
furniture, golden tones on others.
A combination of blues, greens, lavenders
is a variant of the analogous approach
to color in decorating an interior.

Color. Complementary schemes are sharp and decisive, make avant-garde rooms look even more so, and give an up-to-date appearance to settings, such as that at left, in which primarily period pieces are used. To compose one, refer again to the color wheel and choose colors exactly opposite. In these two cases the contrast is afforded by pairing red with yellow-green. Purple and yellow, green and red are other examples of complementary schemes which should always be confined to two colors.

Color. Triadic schemes relate well to conventional, traditionally inspired furnishings, are based, as the name implies, on three colors (often considered the maximum that should be used in a single room). To pick them correctly use the color wheel again and settle for all of the primary colors (labeled 1) or secondary or tertiaries, all numbered accordingly. The simplest of all triadic schemes: red, yellow, and blue has been selected in the case of both the contemporary settings here. Paler tones of the same shades would work very effectively in rooms that are more closely linked to tradition.

Color. Neutral schemes do not depend upon the color wheel but make use of what are known as the "no-color" colors: beiges and grays, taupes and browns, off-whites and gunmetals. Interesting textures: straw-like materials, strong wood grains, woven fabrics with a tweedy look, floor coverings with a sense of depth, are essential to avoid monotony. Backgrounds such as these are the perfect foil for modern paintings with decisive color, accessories with more than the usual amount of brilliance (piles of clashing pillows, for example), and the brightly colored backs of books. Restful and serene, they are endowed with a certain amount of urbanity that makes them seem most comfortably at home with furnishings which are very much of today or under a Japanese influence.

Color. Creams and ivory, oyster and bone and all of the other off-white tones have recently earned their place as basic colors for a room's scheme. Made possible— and even practical—by the introduction of new finishes on fabrics and easy-to-maintain combinations of fibers for floor coverings, such schemes have a luxurious look that makes them extremely stylish.

Then, too, the simplicity of an off-white
scheme makes permissible the use of
reasonably ornate furniture and
accessories, setting these apart like jewels.
As with other neutral color plans, white
schemes also invite the injection of
artwork of unusually strong character.
As far as period goes, however, as the
two settings here indicate, white is
equally at home with traditional or modern.

Color. White with a single brilliantly sharp color added is another color approach increasing in popularity. It is easy to formulate, and its striking effectiveness can do much to distract from and rejuvenate tired furnishings.

CONVERSATION PIT. A
seating group that is dropped
below the regular floor level of
the rest of the room. Offers
a sense of seclusion for those
occupying the sofa units
that are invariably built
right into this pit.

COROMANDEL. A dark wood, found in the Far East, where it is used for furniture—very often lacquered. Most memorable of all are the tall, dark, and handsome screens with intricately detailed scenes. Rare, rich in color and detail, such a screen dominates and dramatizes almost any setting.

CORNICE. The top finish or crowning glory of a
piece of furniture or even the front of a building.
Or, as above, reiterating a usage of the eighteenth
century: an extended box which conceals curtain
and drapery rods. It can also cover bulbs for
indirect lighting.

CORNY. Embarrassingly unsophisticated. Results
from too dedicated a devotion to reproducing
down to the last itsy-bitsy detail the interiors of our
colonial ancestors—forgetting that, in every period,
people do depart from overly precise patterns
of their own time.

COUNTRY LOOK.
Appearing equally as often in the city, this particular style is currently the decorator's delight. A comfortable blend of casual elements borrowed from country houses of France and England, it takes on a twentieth-century look when modified by sharp modern color schemes and contemporary furniture arrangements like that seen at left.

CREWEL. It has been called by one practitioner of this recently revived type of embroidery "cruel" work. Despite the diligence it demands it has remained a favored style of handiwork through four centuries. Originated in England, many patterns were strongly influenced by fabric designs imported from India. Rug at right is modernized version.

69

d

DANTE CHAIR. First done in Italy during the Renaissance, it became particularly popular in seventeenth-century Spain. A reproduction of the second type is seen above.

DECAL. Thin paper printed with designs that can be transferred to china or chests, as above. In early eighteenth-century America a substitute for painted decoration.

DECOY. Realistic portraits of sitting ducks (or sometimes standing ones) used by our ancestors to lure the real thing within gunshot. Today accepted just as decoration.

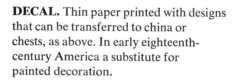

DIRECTOIRE. Early nineteenth-century French style which favored classical motifs derived from the ancient cultures of Greece and Rome. Simple, restrained, and charming.

DOCUMENT. Antique source from which modern reproduction is developed. It can be entirely different from the final product. Here, old jugs inspire a new fabric design.

DRAPERY. Window dressing term referring to the top layer of the treatment. The underneath hangings are called under-curtains. It is incorrect to refer to these as drapes.

e

EAMES. A living designer, first name Charles, best known to the general public for this popular chair that bears his name. Seat and back are molded of plywood.

ECLECTIC. Decorating technique of mixing furniture and accessories from past and present periods, and from many areas of the world. All three rooms pictured here blend modern American with old French. All include big paintings in an abstract style. But, because proportions vary, the resulting look is, in each case, quite different.

ELEGANT. Exuding an air of restrained luxury combined with fastidious taste. Implies the use of expensive materials such as the marble wall and floor, fur rug, silk upholstery used here. The final effect is, however, not overly rich because of the lack of clutter.

74

EMBROIDERIES. Enjoying a revival of popularity for decorative effect are many variations of the art of needlework. They can be hung on a pole, as this one is, or properly framed. Whether conventional or contemporary, their handmade quality provides a pleasant foil particularly for today's standardized furniture.

EMPIRE. Style virtually invented at the behest of Napoleon in the early nineteenth century. On the massive side, it made the most of rich woods, metal mountings, and classical details like the columns on this table.

ENAMEL. Usually applies to the process of adding colored decoration to small metal objects, then baking it on. Alternately refers to a hard, satiny finish that is applied to wooden furniture to add color.

EPÈRGNE. Split-level centerpiece that will hold flowers and/or fruit in separate compartments. This one is in Louis XV style with English lead crystal hand-cut bowls and silver. Simpler versions come in porcelain, pottery.

FABERGÉ. A Russian jeweler of French descent by the name of Carl who concocted exquisitely jeweled bibelots like figures, bird cages, boxes using gold, enamel, precious gems. Lived from 1846 to 1920.

ÉTAGÈRE. French word for open shelves whether standing on the floor or hanging on the wall. Restrained contemporary version would afford attractive display space for a selection of collector's items.

FFF. An abbreviation of fine French furniture, that which was designed in the reigns of Louis XV, Louis XVI. Very expensive, very beautiful, and considered to be the epitome of "rich girl's taste."

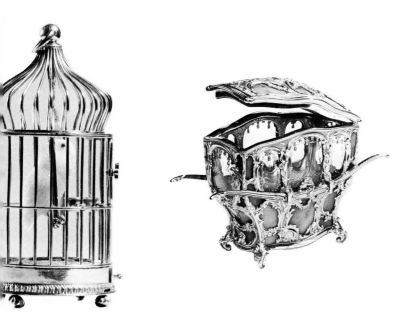

FACADE. Architectural expression referring to the front face of a building; can also be applied to the same portion of a chest. It might be printed, as here, carved, covered with paint, plain wood.

FAMILY ROOM. Updated expression to designate today's replacement for the back parlor, an informal setting arranged for casual living, family fun, easy entertaining. Once known as a rumpus room or recreation room, it serves the same purpose despite the recent change in its name.

FAR EAST FEELING. The atmosphere
that results when objects touched by
the culture of the East—particularly Japan
and China—are added to a room. Above:
pillows of the simple blue and white
print Japanese laborers wear, a delicate
screen over the sofa, a bamboo plant
characteristic of that country add exotic
notes to understated furniture. Chairs,
table that interpret classical Chinese
designs—rather than the accents—give
special air to the setting at right.

FAUX-BOIS. Literally means false wood.
The grain may be photographed,
printed, or even painted on a different
material. Fabric is so treated (above),
also wallpaper.

FAUTEUIL. Upholstered armchair in any
of the French styles. Similar to the *bergère*
described on page 35 but the sides under
the arms are open, not fully upholstered.

FIBER. Any thin thread used in weaving:
whether of glass, silk, cotton, or synthetic.
The word is, however, strongly associated
with woven grasses and reeds like the
hangings which form canopy over the
bed, left.

FILIGREE. Openwork pattern, pierced from metal or occasionally made of wood. Has wonderful light-filtering qualities whether used at windows or for lanterns.

FLOCK. Powdered wool applied to wallpaper in a design to make it look—and also feel—like cut velvet. Now can be imitated in a washoffable plastic sheeting.

FLAME STITCH. Swirling design woven into upholstery fabrics, adapted from a traditional Hungarian needlework stitch. Most frequently in a bright color on neutral ground.

FLOOR COVERINGS. Basic element in the decoration of a room. Whether plain or patterned, wall-to-wall or shaped to cover a small area, very often these can set the atmosphere of a room. They are subject to more variations than at any time in the past. Even plain carpeting is often given an unusual twist as above where two brilliant colors meet. Modern patterns, too, as at left, are more apt to be bold than controlled.

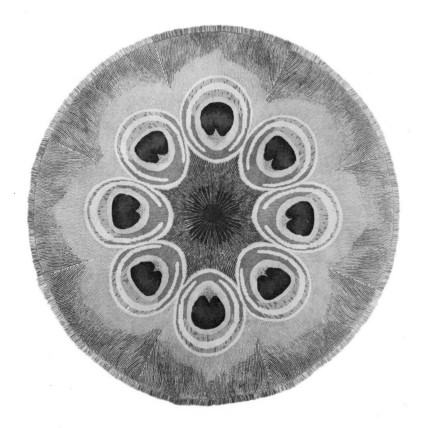

Floor Coverings. Mellow tones of old orientals
are much appreciated for their subtly aged quality
which glows when combined with contemporary
colors and furnishings. When, as here, a precious rug
supplies the only pattern in the room, its importance
and value are emphasized. Antique rugs from
other areas of the world: fuzzy neutrals tinged with
orange from Morocco, pale pastels fabricated
at Aubusson in France with a flat needlepoint
technique, and muted colored, carved temple rugs of
old China are equally prized for the distinction
they can give a room. When the floor covering
becomes that important it can contribute, as it has
here, the theme for the color scheming of a room.
On priceless examples as much of the pattern
as possible should be permitted to show and left
completely free of furniture pieces.

Floor Coverings. Sharp shades of modern patterned rugs
can provide a vivid exclamation point of interest in a room.
Whether worked with a thick-piled, flat surface as at left
or fuzzy, long-haired technique as below, they are best suited
for use in small areas where they may provide a focal point
for a grouping of furniture. It is permissible to place them on
top of plain carpets, or as is more usually done, on a
hard-surfaced floor whether of wood or some other material.
Strictly a twentieth-century addition to the vocabulary
of design, they share one thing in common with patterned rugs
of the past: where the design is strong, it should be permitted
to be the dominant, if not the only pattern in any room
where used. These are called either accent or area rugs.

Floor Coverings. Hard surfaces, whether man-made (left) or of natural materials (the slate, above) play an increasingly interesting role in interior decoration. Among the more intriguing developments of recent years have been vinyl tiles, printed, plain, in bright colors and clear ones and ofttimes imitating almost to perfection the work of nature. Travertine tiles of this plastic, like those used at the left, must be touched to distinguish them from the real thing. The increasing trend toward leaving much of a floor bare has focused interest on floors of this type. Real marble, glass mosaic, and wood parquet are now also making a comeback.

Floor Coverings. Textures of many types are another device used to call attention to floors. The shaggy look of a rug such as this one is an example. Others have carved borders and designs cut into two or even three depths of the pile. They are, however, noticeably less demanding than patterned rugs of any vintage, old or new.

FOLK ART. Crafts identified with
unsophisticated cultures but sufficiently
interesting to warrant inclusion in a
decorating plan. Seen above: bed-covering
and rug from our own Southwest;
wall hanging from South Seas.

FORMAL. Decorating plan arrived at
with quiet precision, luxurious materials.
For success, demands superb housekeeping
with everything in place. Tinged with
tradition rather than contemporary
casualness.

FRAME. Wooden structure on which a chair or sofa is made. Sometimes completely covered over with upholstery; other times portions of the frame are exposed, as above, treated in a decorative fashion.

FREE FORM. One which does not follow any standard shape but flows in curves that are unrelated to the circles, ovals, and spheres with which we are familiar. Much liked in the early days of modern design for tabletops; now confined to experimental settings like this boy's room.

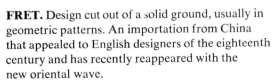

FREE STANDING. Furniture that floats in the center of a room rather than lining up along a wall. To do so successfully, it must be attractive on all four sides. Cabinets are used in this fashion as are sofas.

FRET. Design cut out of a solid ground, usually in geometric patterns. An importation from China that appealed to English designers of the eighteenth century and has recently reappeared with the new oriental wave.

FUN. Word bandied about by professional designers and decorators when discussing the off-beat elements in a room which may bring a smile or even a laugh. Imaginative, tricky, sometimes even toy-like (one architect hangs kites in his living room), they are happy additions to a room and serve to add a warm touch of humanity.

FUNCTIONAL. Furniture that performs more than the obvious purposes. Two cases in point: an armoire that contains a refrigerator; a bed equipped with a table and lamp that slide back to the headboard for working in bed. More strictly: pieces pared down to working parts.

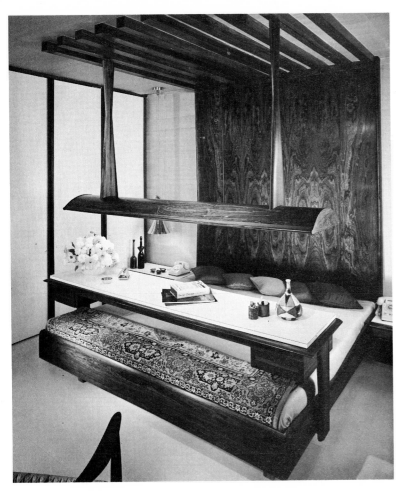

FUR. Luxury note finding a firm place in home fashions. May appear as upholstery, floor covering, throw, or pillow. Many recent examples are fakes, manufactured by man.

93

g

GADROON. Ornamental band of oval shapes placed side by side and rising above the surface of the object they decorate. Enhances simple silver platters, tabletops.

GALLERY. Miniature railing forming a finish around the top of a cabinet or table. Or, a long, narrow passageway especially designed for the best display of works of art.

GALLEY. Long and narrow, again, but with a totally different purpose. Named after the restricted quarters occupied by the cooking equipment on a ship, kitchens of this shape lend themselves to decorative open shelves.

GALLOON. Braids and tapes of various widths that put the finishing touch on upholstered chairs and sofas, or appear as edgings along the sides and bottoms of draperies or curtains. The patterns are woven in.

GEOMETRIC. Patterns based on the symbols of higher mathematics can include plus and minus signs, ovals, circles, squares, and the like. Because of the abstract nature of these, they blend with other types of prints.

GIRONDOLE. Originally meant a wall bracket for candles, often with a mirror behind. Later the mirror came into its own; the candles surrounded it. Traditionally, the mirror rounds out decidedly in the center.

GOTHIC. Derived from a thirteenth-century architectural tradition restated in mid-nineteenth-century terms, such motifs as arches crept briefly into the vocabulary of furniture design (as in the chair at left). Although they have limited application to today, such pieces are intriguing examples of the vagaries of interior design.

JANE Avril

GRAPHIC ART. Drawings, etchings, engravings, and other works of art meant for reproduction—posters are especially popular now.

GREEK KEY. Specific motif of repeated square hooks woven into tapes, carved into moldings. Adapted freely from Greek sources.

GRILLE. Openwork metal or wood grating used at a door or window and, today, also employed as a room divider because it makes possible a very subtle sense of separation.

HALL CLOCK. Alternate for grandfather clock, applies to any tall timepiece encased in a cabinet. Modern designs are joining the ranks of traditional period pieces.

GUNMETAL. Alloy of which cannons were made. Worked into accessories during the seventeenth century when its dull, tarnished look was liked.

HANGING SHELVES. Cliché of the contemporary decorating scene. These shelves which serve as a catch-all for controlled clutter may well go down in history as the hallmark of mid-twentieth-century rooms. On them, books share space with souvenirs, art objects play a part as well as plants. They are the focal point of many modern rooms.

Hanging shelves are capable of infinite variation, as may be seen in the four examples here. Poles can be attached to the wall, brackets hung out from these on which to place the shelves. Alternately, the poles can be placed either eight or ten inches from the wall and brackets fitted in toward the wall. A single shelf, even one with drawers, can be imbedded into plaster to give the impression of floating in the air. Bedrooms are as hospitable to such arrangements as is a living room, library, or dining area.

Hanging shelves are the ideal solution for a study space, whether planned for an adult or a child. A wider working shelf can be worked into the scheme either jutting out into the room or parallel to the wall. Working materials as well as books can occupy nearby open shelves.

HITCHCOCK. Chair named after its American maker, painted to resemble rosewood, stenciled with powdered gold fruit and flowers; still being manufactured in Connecticut.

HEPPLEWHITE. London cabinetmaker working in the mid to late eighteenth century, popularized satinwood and delicate painted finishes, reacted against earlier heaviness.

HIBACHI. Multipurpose stove invented by Japanese to heat people, places, *and* food. Miniature translations from metal originals are useful for heating up hors d'oeuvres.

HOUND'S TOOTH. Tweedy type of check with ragged edges favored for clothing but adopted for use in interiors because of its ruggedly masculine look. Usually black and white as shown above.

HUNT TABLE. Serving table in a semicircular shape, a congenial gathering place for imbibers after the hunt was over. Good for a buffet, for one person standing in center can serve all. Converts to working desk.

i **ILLUMINATED CEILING.** Dropped from the top of the room, lit from above with a series of bulbs, such ceilings can be made of white and colored plastic panels as this one is or of glass or even of metal grilles and grates which resemble normal egg cartons.

INDOOR GARDEN.
Replacement for more
conservative conservatories of
earlier periods, these are now
turning up in more or less
elaborate fashion in all kinds
of informal rooms. Outdoor
elements used here to make
the plants seem in place:
lantern made for a garden,
porcelain tables, brick seats.

INDIAN. Most exotic of all
cultures contributing interest
to present-day rooms.
Intricately woven and gold-
shot cloth; statuettes and boxes
of brass are unexpectedly rich
and rewarding touches when
found in modern rooms.

INDIVIDUALITY. Most
admired and admirable quality
that can be added to
decoration, for it implies the
exertion of a well-developed
personal taste for which there
can be no suggested substitute.
Expressed well in room
at right.

INTERNATIONAL STYLE. Much appreciated by architects of all nations, this modern approach to design is mostly the work of men of that profession. Use of materials favored for building (like metal and glass) results in a look that is amenable to contemporary architecture, seems to supplement rather than to replace or interfere with it.

ITALIANATE. Synonymous with free-thinking, free-wheeling, free-form when it comes to the arts of decoration. Since the early 1950s, the Italian designers have contributed a kind of vim, vigor, and imagination that is unparalleled elsewhere in the world, and, consequently, have had an influence on the decorative arts everywhere in the Western world. Some aspects of this style seen at left and above: unusual lamps whether standing or hanging; curvilinear, molded chairs; decorative cocktail tabletops; slick tile floors; suspended shelves; unusual ceramic shapes for ornamentation.

JAPANESE INFLUENCE. Antidote to the present-day trend toward overdecoration. Simple, natural materials with a minimum of color but a maximum of texture; restraint in the use of accessories (the emphasis put on one particular handsome screen or scroll rather than on a plethora of items) are characteristics that can be happily translated into terms of Western decor. Resulting simplicity—below.

j

KACHINA DOLLS. Beaded and feathered child's toy made by Indian tribes of the Southwest (New Mexico and Arizona), recently accepted by adults as collector's items.

KAKEMONO. Hanging vertical scroll pictures which can be rolled up for storage. It is a Japanese custom to switch them with the four seasons just for a change of scene.

KAS. Imposing, if primitive, type of cupboard typical of the Dutch-American colonists of New York State and the Delaware Valley. Usually paneled and painted with garlands of fruit and flowers.

(COURTESY MUSEUM OF MODERN ART)

KING SIZED. Big bed suited to the bigger people who are populating the world today. Once only available on special order, these oversized sleeping units are now generally available and measure twenty-two inches longer, five inches wider than standard size.

KLISMOS. Classic chair of Greek origin, often pictured on Golden Age urns. Old versions were probably bronze. Modern reinterpretation is made of wood, leather.

KNOLE SOFA. Earliest known type of upholstered sofa, it originated in Elizabethan England, was much admired and imitated by Italian furniture makers of later centuries, continues its popularity in our own time.

1

LACQUER. Furniture finish first done in the Orient, enthusiastically taken up by English and French of the eighteenth century. Traditional examples were often heavily ornamented in gilt and color; modern versions can be plain.

LADDER BACK. Backs of chairs which have a series of horizontal supports, one above another, resembling the steps of a ladder. Found on everything from Spanish examples to modern Danish and including Early American.

LAVEBO. Washbowl, often with a water supply—even possibly a fountain. Fascinating place to put a plant. Mostly made of porcelain or pottery and hung on the wall.

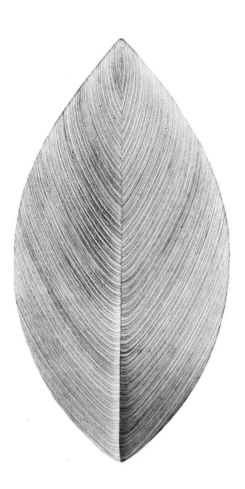

LAMINATE. Process of putting thin layers of materials together under pressure and also heat. When this is done to wood, and it is then sliced down, decorative graining such as seen on the tray above can result. The identical procedure can weld decorative sheets between pieces of clear plastic and produce an intriguing design: see the screen right.

LINENFOLD. Carved motif confined within panels. Descended from Gothic times, it apes the look of folded linens. Most frequently executed in oak, it may be found on the backs of chairs, the fronts of cupboards.

LECTERN. Stand-up reading desk, at one time intended for perusing the Bible; now appears on lecture platforms and does heavy duty in the home supporting dictionaries.

LITTLE NOTHING. Fashion term taken over by interior designers to indicate a severe restraint in the selection and number of furnishings and accessories. All non-essentials are barred, but the injection of such dramatic notes as large, brilliant abstract paintings, important sculptures, carefully planned spotlighting, over-sized plants in pristine containers, help avoid the impression of austerity.

LUMINOUS. Walls illuminated by bulbs concealed by panels of a translucent material such as plastic or glass that is textured or even tinted. Excellent device for brightening a dark corner such as that seen at right. In limited use at the present time but much touted as an up-and-coming trend of the future by lighting engineers who point out the mood-making possibilities of splashing a wall with vari-colored light.

m

MAUVE DECADE. Last one in the nineteenth century, left its mark on interior design with golden oak paneling, heavily embroidered hangings, painted moldings, flocked paper, heavily tufted comfortable chairs, patterned rugs, and—of course—that violet shade, mauve.

MÉLANGE. Mixture of many unrelated elements. Case in point: the collection of small sculptures at left that range from primitive to sophisticated, come from all parts of the world. In a broader sense, descriptive of the contents of a room like that below which combines modern sofa, French antiques, coffee table of the twenties.

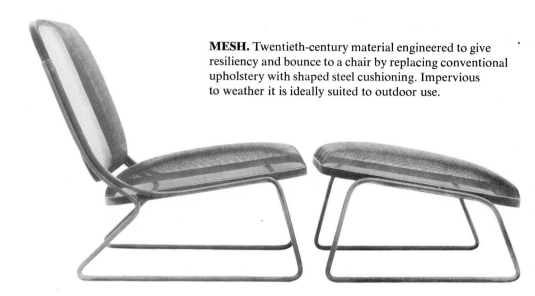

MESH. Twentieth-century material engineered to give resiliency and bounce to a chair by replacing conventional upholstery with shaped steel cushioning. Impervious to weather it is ideally suited to outdoor use.

MIES CHAIR. Classic of all modern chairs, it was designed by an architect, Mies van der Rohe, and originally exhibited in Barcelona, Spain, in 1927. It is still being made in the United States and is esteemed by modernists as one of the great designs of all time. It is chrome and leather.

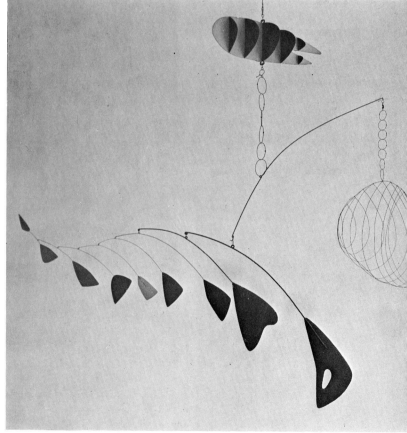

(COURTESY MUSEUM OF MODERN

MOBILE. Abstract sculpture that moves when touched by a breeze or the human hand. It may dangle from the ceiling, as this one does, or hang on a post. "Invented" by the artist Alexander Calder in the 1930s, the principle has been both imitated and enlarged upon.

MODERN. Style of decorating peculiar to the mid-twentieth century. It does not exclude pieces from the past but manages to give old things a new look by placing them in proximity to more modern designs and arrangements as in this corner conversation area where antique stools cluster around a contemporary coffee table. This forthright mixing of periods is very characteristic.

Modern. Restraint and a rejection of fussiness distinguishes this present-day fashion in decor. Plain carpeting, plain painted walls, simple pull-back draperies keep the handsome French pieces in the room at right from seeming overwhelmingly formal. Addition of modern art: painting over the desk, metal sculpture on the coffee table are other elements that designate this as a room of today rather than from some earlier era. Bookshelves built-in along a facing wall and revealed only in the reflection of the large mirror over the sofa contribute further to a completely contemporary impression despite the emphasis on the French period furniture.

Modern. The revolution in color which took place in the 1950s is partially what gives a modern look to American interiors. Conservatism and caution have gone down the drain, and present-day interiors take on a brilliance never seen in any country before. This freedom to use strong straight color (a true red, an intense blue, an undiluted yellow) is unprecedented in the history of interior decoration and therefore correctly referred to as "modern." This attitude will unquestionably continue to characterize color attitudes of the future, whether in rooms fitted out with period or contemporary pieces.

Modern. Furniture that looks built-in, taking on an architectural flavor is part of the modern approach to decorating. Shelves, whether single ones or a wall of them, may go down in history as an identifying mark of our own particular period. What goes on the shelves is also pretty typical, for books rarely stand alone but share space with propped pictures, collector's items, simple souvenirs and curios. This trend offers an unparalleled opportunity to achieve that most valued quality in interior decorating: a highly individual and personal touch. The impact these shelf arrangements have makes them dominate the whole room.

Modern. Fitting closed storage and concealed sound equipment into a wall of shelves is an extension of the comparatively recent concept explored on the preceding pages. Although the general effect is of a custom-made, specially planned wall, this particular example, like many others, was made up from ready-made units.

MOLDED CHAIR. Chair based on a frame that is molded or pressed into shape rather than, as in former ages, glued and nailed. Most are pleasingly sculptural.

MODULE. Standard measurement—applicable to architecture, and now to furniture design. Makes it possible to fit chests together to make them appear built-in.

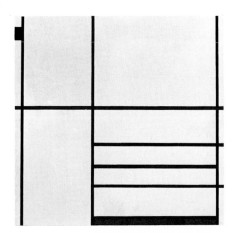

(COURTESY MUSEUM OF MODERN ART)

MONDRIAN. Twentieth-century painter whose asymmetric compositions of black lines and bright blocks of red, yellow, and blue on a white ground have had a profound effect on interior design, suggesting fabrics and furniture arrangement, as well as actual duplication, seen here, on a kitchen wall.

MOORISH. Spanish style much under the influence of North Africa, most appreciated in the 1880s when the room below was done, and seemingly in for a revival in the 1960s. As ornate as the eclectic rooms of the Victorian era but different in that over-all design inspiration derives consistently from one particular source.

MOSAIC. Small squares of colored glass set in cement frequently in a pattern. Decorative asset on walls and floors of Early Christian and Byzantine churches where it first appeared and equally effective in the same areas in many contemporary houses.

M̲OTIF. Design theme reiterated in several forms
d different materials throughout a room's
eme. This emphasis makes it the dominant
ture of the setting, as with the roses shown
ove and the keys seen right.

MURAL. Picture applied to a wall as part of the over-all plan of a room. May be painted; in this day and age much more apt to be printed on paper. Although the subject matter ranges from caricatures of celebrities like those above to scenic landscapes as at left, a three-dimensional effect is a prominent characteristic.

n

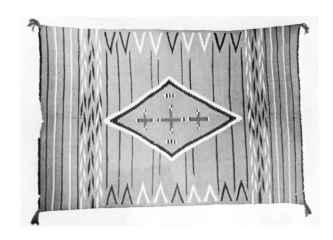

NAVAJO. Blanket hand-woven by a specific Indian tribe of the Southwest portion of the United States, its geometric patterns and neutral colors make it suitable for use as a rug. Old examples are rare, very expensive.

NEAR EASTERN INFLU-ENCE. Source of exotic atmosphere for those who do not choose to go all the way to the Far East for inspiration, but borrow instead from the Mediterranean shores of Asia, Africa. Much use of grilles.

NEEDLEPOINT. Any embroidery stitch used on canvas. Can be large *(gros)* or tiny *(petite)*. Modern versions show up as pillows, placques, and pictures, rugs and the coverings of chairs.

NICHE. Set-back recess in a wall made especially to receive either a small object—a statue, for example—or a larger, more extensive one such as a bed. Emphasizes importance of object so displayed.

NOSTALGIA. Liking for a look backward. Good description for the sentiments of those addicted to authentic period rooms or to collections which put an emphasis on sentimental mementos of times of the past.

 OBELISK. Tall, tapering, towering, monumental shape. Stone ones guarded Egyptian temples of antiquity. Imitations in porcelain or in glass, colored, clear, or incised with decoration, have become collector's items.

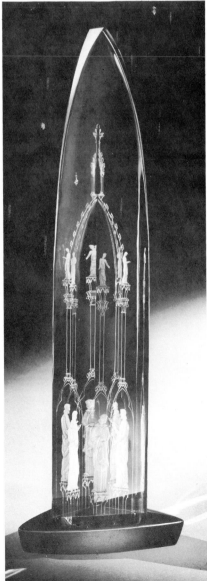

OCCASIONAL FURNI-TURE. Odd stools, chests, tables, chairs in a different and most often much more decorative style than the main furnishings of a room. Carved or given a painted design, the very oddity of these pieces makes them acceptable additions to rooms of any period persuasion—whether modern or old.

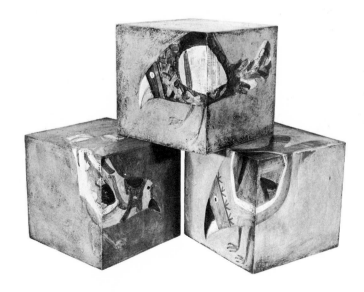

ONE PATTERN LOOK.
Fashion for using a single
design in all areas of a room:
walls, window treatment,
furniture coverings. Perfect
device for unifying unmatched

pieces. Seen above is a
variation: the same pattern
appears throughout in white
on blue but walls are blue
on white.

OP ART. Paintings made up of lines placed in such a way that they seem to move when regarded by the viewer for any prolonged length of time.

OPEN FLOOR PLAN. Elimination of conventional walls between rooms results in this kind of situation where living room, dining room, and possibly the foyer become a single large area broken up only by the furniture arrangement.

ORIENTAL ACCENTS.
Items of smallish size but
great character that spice an
interior with seasonings from
the Far East. Seen to the right:
Japanese lacquer tray, Thai
silver compote, Chinese statue.
Such a judicious selection
flavors a room without
becoming cloyingly exotic
or unusual.

139

ORMOLU. Brass or copper ornaments, gilded and added to various types of chests to lend an air of sumptuousness. Still another contribution from eighteenth-century France.

OTTOMAN. An upholstered footrest accompanying a chair, or, an armless and backless seat that is very low. Takes its name from this latter type popularized during the Turkish influence on eighteenth-century Europe.

p

PAISLEY. Patterns originally embroidered on scarves from Kashmir in India, later copied by Scotch mills, now printed onto upholstery and curtain fabrics, woven into rugs.

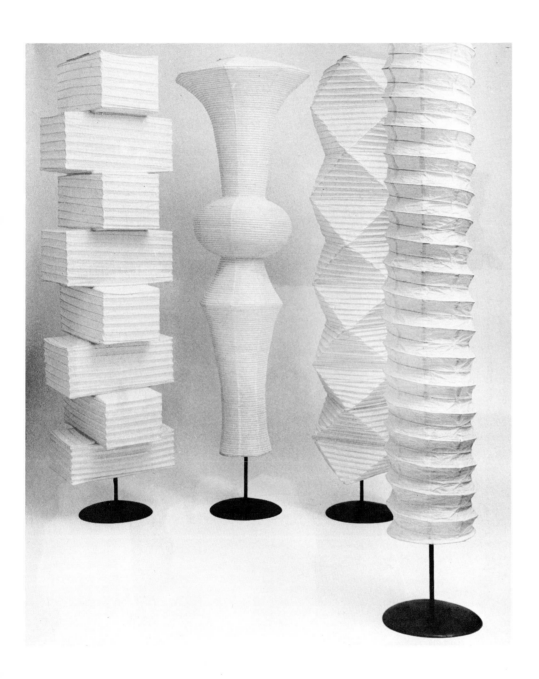

PAPER. Plays a surprisingly and an increasingly important role in contemporary interior decoration. One example: the standing lamps above, a modern reinterpretation of the traditional Japanese paper lantern. Hand-printed draperies of paper were part of the nineteenth-century English scene, and a new version (knitted paper) seen right, is making a bid as a curtain material.

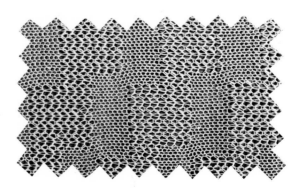

PAPERWEIGHTS. Any objects weighty enough to hold down a pile of papers, but glass ones (particularly of French origin) attract a horde of collectors—see above.

PAPIER-MACHE. Just paper, wetted down and mixed into pulp, then formed into decorative objects and colored on the surface. Traditional Indian figure and a modern Danish tray, shown right, are versions of it.

PARQUET. Decorative effect achieved by fitting short slices of wood into an attractive flooring pattern. Recently appropriated by designers for tabletops or whole tables.

PASS-THROUGH. Broken-through portion of a wall fitted with a shelf on one or both sides which facilitates service between kitchen and dining area. It should be placed high enough to conceal the cooking equipment.

PATTERN ON PATTERN. Fashion for playing one pattern off against another in a single setting. Currently the decorator's delight because it takes professional skill to blend unrelated designs. It can result, as at left, in a room containing five totally different patterns, a most intriguing medley of motifs.

PATTERN PLACEMENT. Much more usual—and usable— style in which a single pattern is selected and serves as a clue to the color scheming and planning of a setting. The striking black and white print of the canopy above is, for example, lightly tinged with red, suggesting the accent color to enliven the basic black and white.

Pattern Placement. Applied to a large piece of furniture, a sofa, for example, a print can accomplish one of two purposes. It can suggest a whole new color scheme for a room, or, if carefully selected, can act as a catalyst blending together the already existing elements. In either event it should be bold, positive, and with a clearly defined color scheme. In this case, lavender and blue blossoms suggested the fabric on the easy chairs which combine the two shades in an almost unnoticeable stripe. The yellow-green of the French *bergères* also shows up faintly in the pattern. The rug, a tweed, combines all of the colors. Stripes and tweedy types of textiles are non-competitive to more distinct and more illustrative patterns, and work effectively with them.

Pattern Placement. Brilliant accent rug on the floor of the bedroom, left, dictated the off-beat color scheme of blues and purples sparked by red. Matching quilted spread and plain drapery pick up the palest tones, while the more vivid ones appear on three chairs—each of them different. Rug unifies these disparate elements.

Wall covering on a large scale adds interest to a one-room apartment, controls its color scheming by suggesting red for vitrine, carpet, table apron, and repetition of design on the chair cushions. Geometric nature of braid trimming daybed covers (the only other pattern in the room) does not compete with stylized floral.

Pattern Placement. Window wall becomes the dominating element in this room because of the distinctly printed window shades which, as with the patterns preceding, impose the colors upon the room. Fabric window shades, recently become popular, make this concept a possibility for even the simplest kind of room. A stripe which blends, without matching precisely, and a textured tweed on the sofa are other patterns included here, but, again, their quiet nature does not distract from the unrealistically colored but carefully drawn floral design.

Pattern Placement. Coffee tabletop is the *pièce de résistance* here. Made of mosaic in an abstract design, it reiterates all of the blues and lavenders in the room, including those of the rya rug hung like a painting above the fireplace. Because of its abstract nature, it supplements rather than interferes with the sofa design.

PEDESTAL. Supporting block for a statue or base for a table. In the latter case it eliminates a mass of legs. Same central support has, of late, even been introduced for use on small occasional seating pieces.

PEGBOARD. Modern building material frequently applied to interior walls. It is punctuated with holes into which one may fit pegs on which to hang anything from art to pots and pans and even mops.

PHYFE. Among the most famous of American cabinet makers, Duncan lived and worked in New York City during the early decades of the nineteenth century. He favored lyre-shaped backs for chairs, curved cornucopia-shaped legs for sofas. Early work like this chair is in the Adam and Sheraton tradition. Later pieces got heavier.

153

PIER GLASS. Narrow, elongated wall-hung mirror, almost full length, suspended between two windows or above an extremely low console-type table. Elaborately framed ones were popular during the Victorian age.

PILASTER. Fake, flattish column applied to a wall but, unlike a column, supporting nothing and simply added for decorative effect, as next to the hallway door below. Fully equipped with a base and capital.

PLANTER. Receptacle especially designed to receive the potted plants no self-respecting room is without these days. Can be built-in like this trough or only large enough to contain a single example.

PLASTICS. Sturdy, easy-to-maintain wonder materials, made by man, they turn up on walls, floors, tabletops, and even in a shapely transparent chair on metal base.

PLATFORM. Raised area at one end of a room. Minor version of a split level (see page 180), it can add considerable architectural interest to a severe modern room.

PLYWOOD. Building material made up of thin layers or veneers of wood glued together. Since the grains of the layers are usually at right angles to each other, although it is quite thin it is exceptionally strong.

POLE LAMP. Series of light sources suspended from a floor-to-ceiling pole. Intriguing because of its flexibility: the bullet-type shades can be aimed up toward the ceiling, down at a book, or spotting a work of art.

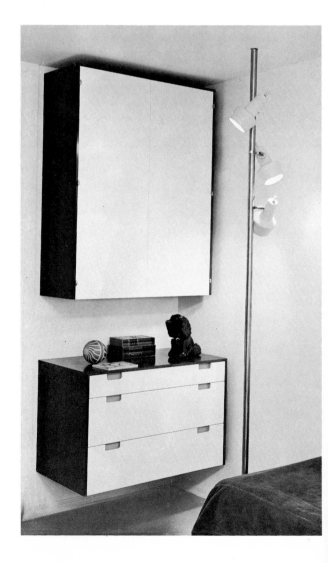

POP ART. Developed in the 1960s to satirize the constant visual distraction imposed on modern man, it derives its inspiration from such sources as popular packaging, road signs, comic strip characters.

POTPOURRI. Like a mélange (page 119), a mad mixture of the kind to be found on the ubiquitous shelves that are a hallmark of twentieth-century decoration. Here, precious ivories keep company with attractive trivia.

POUF. Related to an ottoman but higher and puffier and at times round. These particular piles of pillows are carved of wood, aping the more conventional upholstered ones.

PRE-COLUMBIAN. Arts and artifacts of Central and South America created before Columbus stumbled on this hemisphere. These Peruvian examples are silver, ceramic, gold.

PRIMITIVE. Inspired by unsophisticated cultures, both those of today and those of the past. The fabric right was, for example, inspired by one from native African tribes. Objects, below, are from many areas.

q

QUATREFOIL. Stylized Gothic rendition of a four-leaf clover, here decorating a contemporary clock. A similar three-leaved interpretation is called a trefoil.

QUEEN ANNE. Curvilinear walnut pieces are typical of this eighteenth-century English style that had great influence in America and in Bermuda as well.

r

RATTAN. An American discovery. Rattan commonly carried as ballast on clipper ships between east Indian ports and our own country, constituted a fire menace when dumped out on the docks. One of the volunteers paid to carry it away decided to make a rocking chair from his bundle of poles. Since this event in the mid-nineteenth century, it has attained great popularity.

RÉCAMIER. Early nineteenth-century type of chaise with gracefully curved back, named after the very special French lady who used to recline upon a similar one.

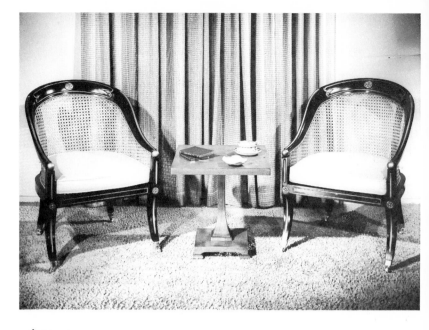

RÉGENCE. French style of the first decades of the eighteenth century. The scale is small, the forms are free and curving. Furniture of the period has an appealing delicacy.

REGENCY. English style of a hundred years later than the French *Régence*. Simple, severe, and under the influence of Greek and Roman classicism. Fairly sturdy in scale.

REPRODUCTION. Precise copy of an authentic antique whether it be a piece of furniture like the one at right that is at Williamsburg or a pattern of a fabric or rug, or even a small accessory of silver or porcelain.

ROCOCO. French words for rock and shell are combined to make this word which describes the kind of design that followed *Régence*. Free, light and curvy it tends toward overornamentation of surfaces on some occasions.

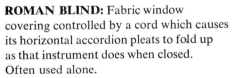
ROMAN BLIND: Fabric window
covering controlled by a cord which causes
its horizontal accordion pleats to fold up
as that instrument does when closed.
Often used alone.

ROOM DIVIDER. Partial wall to replace
the full wall removed in an open floor plan.
Poles serve the purpose, as do cascades of
beads or an open see-through storage unit.

RUSH. Possibly the oldest of furniture materials, for Moses' crib was woven of such reeds. Chair seats made of this material have remained popular since those early origins.

RUSTIC. Deep country look with a woody, stalwart character and a made-by-hand appearance. At its best combined with tweedy homespuns that share the same kind of ruggedness.

RYA RUG. Long-haired, hand-made rug of Finnish descent intended as a blanket, more often used as a rug in our own country but equally suitable as a decorative wall hanging.

SAARINEN. Eero, an architect, gave his name to this very famous chair, an early example of a molded (rather than nailed and glued) chair frame padded with rubber latex.

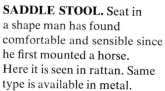

SADDLE STOOL. Seat in a shape man has found comfortable and sensible since he first mounted a horse. Here it is seen in rattan. Same type is available in metal.

SANTO. Image of a saint, primitively carved of wood and finished in manly colors, much valued for decoration today in secular settings.

SAUNA. Setting for a steam bath, Finnish style. Planked with fragrant wood, fitted with comfortable seating. In the country of origin, a roll in the snow is the finale.

SCANDINAVIAN STYLE. Our inheritance from the three small countries of Northern Europe who, along with neighboring Finland, have had a strong influence on contemporary design. In this Swedish home, the furniture is simple but not severe, relieved by curves.

Scandinavian styles differ from one country to the next.
The tightly tailored, neatly tufted chairs and sofas
of Danish designers seem to have a lasting appeal to
American taste. Teak, a favored wood in that country,
also has found a place for itself here. Both are included in
the room, far left. Norwegian design, directly left, is
less sophisticated, pared to the bone of simplicity.
Finnish interiors owe much to the inventiveness of
architect Alvaar Aalto, who designed the room below.
Its woody look reflects Finland's many forests.

SCONCE. Wall bracket of a decorative nature fashioned to hold candles. Later-day interpretations are wired for electricity.

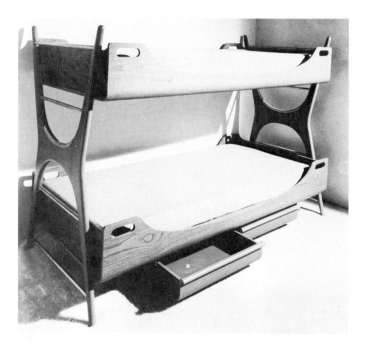

SCROLL. Intricate spiral forms whether woven into a fabric, carved out of wood and serving for the base of a chair or table, or worked in metal to form a grille.

SCULPTURAL. Mid-twentieth-century approach to either carving or molding forms for furniture. Both methods are relied upon to soften the lines of this bunk bed.

SERENE. An atmosphere achieved only by the most discriminating selectivity and best typified by the traditional sparseness—but not severity—of a true Japanese interior with its single flower arrangement, single work of art, and natural textures devoid of much color.

SETTEE. Elongated seating piece with back and arms constructed for the comfort of several persons. Also a shortish sofa.

SHAKER. Christian sect of "shaking Quakers" who in early nineteenth-century New England created a spare functional style.

SHERATON. Along with Chippendale and Hepplewhite, the third of the great eighteenth-century furniture designers. Credited with being the first to trim furniture with china plaques; interested in folded furniture.

SHOJI. Sliding wood and paper panels of Japanese houses. Running from floor to ceiling, they permit privacy but allow light to filter through from room to room. One can be seen at the far right of the room opposite.

SKYLIGHT. Window cut into a ceiling to permit light to filter down from the sky above. In modern houses may be fitted with a plastic bubble which can also be illuminated after dark. At left, plain glass was used.

SPACE PLANNING. Considering all of the architectural assets and deficits as well as the furnishings when decorating. In this tiny room, windows, walls, and ceiling are very important to the over-all effect.

SPACE SAVING. Kind of multi-purpose, double-duty furniture that by performing more than one function leaves room for other essentials. It might be a desk that doubles for dining or a table that expands.

SPANISH. Strong influence on decorating trends of the 1960s, this extremely ornate style affected the look of backgrounds: encouraging the use of tiles on floors and walls and the introduction of carved and metal grilles. Heavy furniture, carved, inlayed, or combined with black iron and brilliant patterned rugs and spreads, are other aspects of this particular trend.

SPARSE. Pared down to the basic essentials with a minimum of both furnishings and accessories, rooms of this sort have more of an intellectual than emotional appeal. Lots of white space, precise but asymmetric placement, touches of black, lend a poster-like look.

SPLIT BAMBOO. Thin strands of bamboo split off of the stalk, woven together with fine threads to create window coverings that filter light with miraculous subtlety. Flexible as fabric, this material may either be made into blinds or fashioned into pleated draperies.

SPLIT LEVEL. Room on planes, a descendant of the dropped living rooms of the thirties where living and dining areas were differentiated by having one placed two or three steps above the other. Actually, an extended platform large enough to encompass elements needed for another activity.

SPOTLIGHT. Borrowed from scenic design, these powerful lights are used at home to focus attention on works of art when they play a starring role in a room. At right, one picks out the gleaming curves of a modern abstract metal sculpture. Other types play up the color values of paintings, revealing all their true colors.

STACKING. Pieces planned to fit one on top of another for condensed storage. Cups and saucers, pitchers and platters and even chairs are formulated in this fashion today.

STORAGE WALL. Built-in cabinets, drawers, desks, and even beds occupying most or all of a wall and designed to care for an individual's (or a family's) possessions.

STRAW. Dried stalks of grain, the earliest type of bedding when shredded and strewn on the floor. More intricate treatments wind up as stools for indoors—or outdoors.

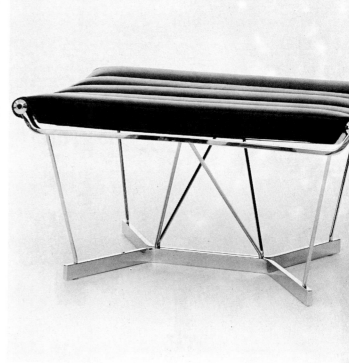

STRUT. Bar that by exerting pressure holds up a bridge, or, in this case, a stool. Engineering principle applied to furniture design results in a slick, industrial look.

STUDIED. Rigid, carefully planned placement that leaves little or no room for a change. The boxes on this open table have, for example, been worked into a composition.

STYLIZED. Motifs that express the essential form rather than the realistic appearance of that which inspired the pattern, as the tulips here that never grew in any garden.

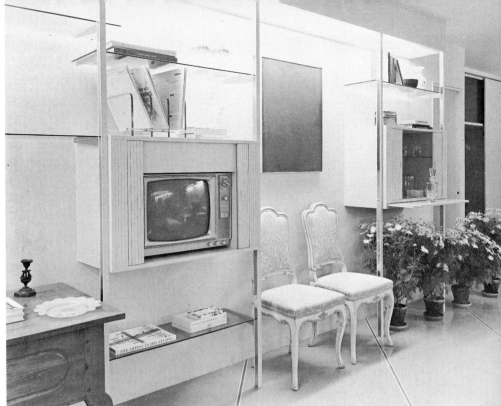

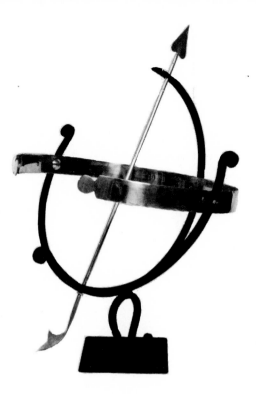

SUNDIAL. Time-telling gadget that ticks off the daytime hours by casting a shadow on a flat plate or cylindrical surface.

SUSPENDED. Floating state of furniture that is free on all sides except at the point where it is supported. Closely related to hanging shelves described on pages 99 to 102.

SWAG. Fabric draped in a looped effect suggestive of the fashion in which a garland of flowers might be hung. Elaborate top treatment for traditional window draperies.

SYMMETRICAL. Balance achieved by relying upon pairs of pieces evenly distributed around a dominating element such as a sofa. Matching tables, matching lamps, matching stools, or pull-up chairs set this way have a correct look that smacks of traditional formality. The principle may be applied to as modern a room as that below, but is more often seen in period settings.

SYNTHETIC. Artificial man-made substitute for a natural material. Ranges from rayons and leather-like plastics to plushy make-believe furs recently produced.

t

TABOURET. Type of stool, no longer sat upon, but serving as a table. Name derives from drum shape; can be made of metal, or porcelain in white or many colors.

TAMBOUR. Flexible door that slides along a groove following the curves of a chest. Made of thin strips of wood glued to canvas; is the roll of a rolltop desk.

TAPESTRY. Hand-woven textile, usually pictorial in design. Dates back to the seventeenth century, when it was popular for chair coverings. Regarded as an art form today. On modern versions abstract design may replace conventionally rendered illustrations.

TATAMI. Ribbon-bound straw mat standard for flooring in a Japanese house where rooms are measured by the number of three-by-six-foot mats required to reach from wall to wall. Stuffed with more straw for resiliency in the land of origin; in our own country plastic-finished for durability.

TESTER. Framework that upholds the canopy on a
four-poster bed. Evolved from the French word for head,
this term expresses what a canopy does—it covers the head.

TÊTE-À-TÊTE. Nineteenth-century seat with chairs facing in opposite directions. Shaped curves give it a sinuous grace that put it back on the twentieth-century scene.

THONET. Austrian furniture designer of the early nineteenth century, earliest fabricator of bentwood chairs of which this is the most famous example.

TIFFANY. American designer renowned for iridescent glass goblets and lamps, vases and the like which reflected the ideas of Art Nouveau.

TOILE. Printed cottons produced at Jouy, France in late eighteenth century composed of realistic pictures of flowers, fruit, people and landscapes.

TOLE. Tin, painted or enameled in deep, rich shades of yellows, reds and greens and formed into various decorative accessories and lamps.

TORCHÈRE. Stand that uphold a light, whether candle, oil or electric. In earlier centuries these stands were perched directly on the floor.

TOPIARY. Tree trimmed into extraordinary shape by a gardener; duplicated in metal (as here) or plastic to add charm to indoor situations.

TRADITIONAL. Style of decorating in which most of the ingredients and many of the principles are taken from the customs and case histories of periods past. An attempt to preserve the spirit of the best that has been done before our own time, but not necessarily a direct duplication of rooms. Colors, art are different.

TRANSITIONAL. Blend of past and present, maintaining the best features of both. Examples of old pieces are authentic and the new concepts injected are equally true to *our own* times. Often ends up by being a cultivated capsule expression of cultures old and new. Expressed irreverently, irrelevantly and without precedents.

TREILLAGE. Latticework for supporting vines. Word is now applied to the kind of decoration rampant in indoor-outdoor rooms which capture the feeling of a garden within four walls. Essential to successful decorating of one of these is the use of trellises such as the wood example at left framing the massed plants or the wallpaper, right, surrounding a room.

TRIPOD. Three-pronged base for supporting either a table or chair. Traditional ancestors of Spanish (right) or English origin suggested more modern interpretations.

TRIVET. Plate warmer placed near a fireplace—also used for keeping a kettle warm. Although once fitted with three, acquired a fourth one in course of development.

TROMPE L'ŒIL. Art of painting a wall or object to fool and confuse the eye—an ancient art revived for today's walls. Foodstuffs, above, on sliding doors and chest and mirror, far right, must be examined carefully for assurance that they are painted rather than real.

TRUNDLE BED. Bed on wheels which fits under another one. Inherited from Gothic times, it is popular now for teen-age rooms.

TUFTING. Upholstering technique in which buttons tie the fabric to the inner stuffing. Results in patterns as those seen below.

TURN-OF-THE-CENTURY. Fashions
of 1900 which have permeated later
design thinking. Flavor captured above.

TURNING. Carpentry term that
describes circular cutting of woods by tools.
Decorative device to support canopies
and tables.

VALENCE. That which tops a drapery treatment. Can be fabric swagged as here, or draped in another fashion or even made of wood.

VENETIAN. Delightfully ornate style of furnishing evolved in that city. Rich and elegant, adds wonderful accent to simple rooms.

VENETIAN BLIND. Window covering of small wood or aluminum slats hung horizontally and strung on a tape so that they can be turned up or down.

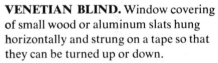

VERTICAL BLINDS. The same principle as that above—but runs up and down, not across. In the example shown fabric replaces wood or metal.

VICTORIAN. Era which took its name from the famed
Queen of England whose purity of taste did not penetrate
into the arts of decoration. Quite the contrary, it
permitted a strange mixture of such unrelated objects
as may be found in the two rooms illustrated here, both
American interpretations of this English fashion.

VICTORIAN INFLUENCE. Flavor that pervades certain rooms today, which, while they do not duplicate the homes of our ancestors, preserve the traditions of chubby chairs, tiny tables, emphasis on bric-a-brac.

VITRINE. Cabinet of French origin that holds curios behind glass-enclosed shelves. For modern collectors, many are equipped with built-in lighting devices, the better to show up the encased precious objects.

WEDGWOOD. English pottery dating from the mid-eighteenth century, prominently associated with tasteful re-creations of classic urns and interesting innovations in wall, table, mantle, and door ornaments.

WALL-HUNG. Still another descriptive term to apply to suspended shelves—even a single one that serves as a telephone table.

WALL TREATMENTS. See page 216 and on.

WEBBING. Basket weave of burlap, at one time an undercover support for upholstery, now brought out in the open and used alone.

WEIRD. Pertaining to witchcraft and the supernatural—tokens and totems of primitive religions which have found a place in the interior decorations of our contemporary homes.

WHAT-NOT. Ornamental shelves meant for holding ornaments. Fancy and fanciful nineteenth-century version of an *étagère*—opener and more intricately carved and conceived.

WHEEL-BACK CHAIR. Back of chair design inspired by a wheel, complete to spokes radiating from the center to a circle or oval. Heritage from eighteenth-century England.

WHIMSEY. Capricious note with a touch of humor that can extirpate the dullness from a dreary room. The lady-like flower holder and the see-through seat are two examples.

WICKER. Thin twig which can be worked into lacy, openwork patterns. Once confined to porch rockers, wicker now finds a well-earned place inside the house.

WINDBELLS. Hung in a window to catch the slightest suggestion of a breeze, these tinkling trinkets appear to have the ability to make it seem cooler even on the hottest day. An inheritance from the Japanese.

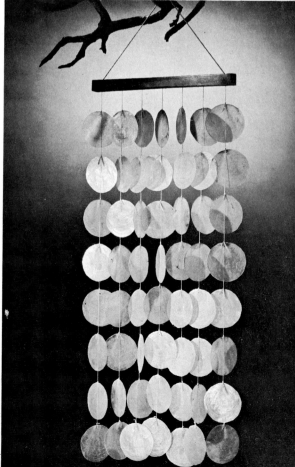

WINDOW SHADES. Far cry from the dull institutional window coverings of another generation, window shades today take on a wholly unexpected gaiety. They may be paper or printed fabric, textured or plain, pull-up in conventional fashion or even pull-down from the top (see directly at the right). Plasticized for easy maintenance, they are as good a method as any of controling light and providing privacy. Four variations are illustrated in the rooms here.

WIRE. Thin metal strands that lend themselves to whimsical designs for either inside or out. Lightweight but sturdy enough.

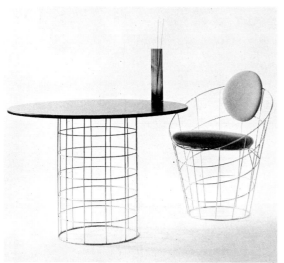

X-BASE. Cross-legged support for stools and tables. Originated by the Greeks (the example near right is taken from an ancient prototype), modernized versions are popular.

Z

ZEBRA. Latest of the wild beasts to enter the home scene. Fabrics that imitate its fur have caught on with the new interest in black and white combinations. There's zebra wood, too (used for paneling above). It takes its name from the strong stripes.

WALL TREATMENTS. Walls occupy
the largest amount of total space in a room.
As a result they set the tone of the
decoration determining whether the wood
will be casual or formal. A slick surface
such as the mirror at left implies a certain
formality despite the room's modernity.
Recent practice permits hanging a painting
directly on the mirrored surface as was
done here. Movable walls of wood-framed
paper like the shoji of a Japanese house
suggest the understated serene blend
of East and West shown below.

color schemes

Wall Treatments. Paper can add more than prettiness, sometimes lends itself to such architectural effects as that at left, where the border not only circles the striped walls but continues over the windows to take the place of a fabric swag. In the setting below, companion papers add interest. One is applied to the walls leading to the dining area, a second plainer plaid in mated colors covers a single wall of the room itself. Other walls are painted the lightest color while window shades match the paper.

Wall Treatments. Wood paneling for walls is subject to infinite variation, can be combined with walls not so treated, and goes particularly well with brick. In degrees of formality ranging from old weathered board taken from barns to the carved panelings of France (called *boiseries*), it can be finished in tones from dark teak and rosewood to the light pine hung in a chevron pattern behind the bed below. Either this or the walnut in the modern house at right provide quiet natural backgrounds against which to play bright color.

Wall Treatments. Fabric-covered walls, a time-honored device in traditional rooms, are putting in an appearance in those of more contemporary character. It looks more extravagant than it is. A simple wood frame can be made to fit the room, then the fabric is nailed to the frame and stretched tightly. In still simpler fashion, curtain rods, top and bottom, can hold the fabric in place, making it removable for cleaning. A traditional chintz, a modern bright red burlap used in the two rooms on these pages illustrate different effects that can be achieved. In the traditional dining room, paneling holds the fabric in place. The burlap is glued to the wall.

ACKNOWLEDGMENTS

Layouts designed by Arnold Hoffmann, Jr.

To the following group of manufacturers, importers, and shops, the author is grateful for photographic material supplied: B. Altman & Co., America House, A La Vieille Russie, Antique Art & Antique Dealers, Armstrong Cork Co., Artes de Mexico, Avard, Basic-Witz Furniture Industries, Baker Furniture Co., Bonniers, Yale Burge, Cabin Crafts, Celanese, Charak, Philip Colleck, Conso Trimming Co., Decorative Imports, Decorators Walk, De Gaal & Walker, Pino L. de Luca, Design Technics, Drexel, Dunbar, Dupal Furniture Co., Foam Latex Rubber Council, French & Co., Ginsberg & Levy, Gorham, Hammacher Schlemmer, Hitchcock Chair Co., House of Spain, Georg Jensen, Edwin Jackson, Herman Kashins, Kittinger, Knoll Associates, Lane Furniture Co., Arthur H. Lee, Macy's, Morrison Imports, Palladio, Paper Plate and Container Institute, Phillips Galleries, Piazza, Harvey Probber, Raymor, Lew Raynes, Royal System, Isabel Scott, James Seeman Studios, Selig, Spanish Trading Center, Sprague & Carleton, W. & J. Sloane, Stockwell Wallpaper Co., David Stockwell, Steuben, John Strauss, Syroco, Tomlinson, Tropi-cal, Thonet, U. S. Plywood, U. S. Rubber, V'Soske, Otto M. Wasserman, Wedgwood.

Appreciation should also be expressed for the cooperation of the interior designers listed below whose work is included in the following pages: Beryl Austrian, Leigh Allen, David Barrett, Braswell-Cook, Baldwin & Machado, John Bedenkapp, Samson Berman, David Eugene Bell, Everett Brown, Alexander Calder, d'Argout Ferguson, Marion Dorn, Mary Dunn, Charles Eames, Eddie Fredericks, Lawrence Fleischman, Augusta Gassner, Alexander Girard, Jeremiah Goodman, Hector Grant, Henriette Granville, Michael Greer, Jack Hartrick, Patricia Harvey, Marjorie Boradaille Helsel, Albert Herbert, Joseph Hoffman, Evelyn Jablow, Vladimir Kagan, Melanie Kahane, John Keal, Virginia Kelly, Paul Krauss, Charles & Camille Lehman, Robert Lindenthal, George Lippart, Alvin Lustig, Jack Macurdy, Jerome Manashaw, Harry Martin, William Parker McFadden, Ed Motyka, Muller-Bachich, Robert Luther Myers, George Nagashima, George Nelson, Geraldine Nicosia, Bengt Nordquist, William Pahlmann, Gary Pizzarelli, Leonard H. Price, Gio Ponti, William Raiser, T. H. Robsjohn Gibbings, Howard Rothberg Perry, Renny Salzman, Astrid Sampe, Harold Schwartz, Staniford Squire, Mrs. Belmont Tobin, Mies van der Rohe, John Van Koert, Robert Walker, Craig Weston, David Whitcomb, John Wisner, Edward Wormley, Tom Yee, May Veronica Yhap.

Also assisting were a group of galleries, museums, and individual artists. They are: American Craftsmen Council, Asia Society, Brooklyn Museum, Henry Ford Museum, Norman LaLiberte, Metropolitan Museum of Art, Mondrian, Museum of American Indian, Julian Stanczak, Stony Point Folk Art Gallery, Bjorn Wiinblad, Winterthur Museum, Tapio Wirkkala.

Also helpful in the compilation of this material were the members of my own staff: Gladys Gough and Michael Landers.